bison

yellow warbler

hairy

elk

mountain bluebird

grizzly bear

buffaloberry

black bear

deermouse

American robin

moose

chorus frog

cattail

mallard duck

red-winged blackbird

river otter

WETLAND SPECIES

beaver

First published in Canada and the United States in 2017
Text and illustration copyright © 2017 Celia Godkin
This edition copyright © 2017 Pajama Press Inc.
This is a first edition.

10 9 8 7 6 5 4 3 2 1

www.pajamapress.ca   info@pajamapress.ca

 Canada Council   Conseil des arts
for the Arts   du Canada

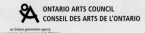 ONTARIO ARTS COUNCIL
CONSEIL DES ARTS DE L'ONTARIO
an Ontario government agency
un organisme du gouvernement de l'Ontario

Canadä

The publisher gratefully acknowledges the support of the Canada Council for the Arts and the Ontario Arts Council for its publishing program. We acknowledge the financial support of the Government of Canada through the Canada Book Fund (CBF) for our publishing activities.

Library and Archives Canada Cataloguing in Publication

Godkin, Celia, author
     The wolves return : a new beginning for Yellowstone National Park
/ Celia Godkin.
ISBN 978-1-77278-011-6 (hardback)

     1. Gray wolf--Reintroduction--Yellowstone National Park--Juvenile
literature. 2. Yellowstone National Park--Juvenile literature. I. Title.

QL737.C22G64 2017   j599.77309787'52   C2016-903703-7

Publisher Cataloging-in-Publication Data (U.S.)

Names: Godkin, Celia, author.
Title: The wolves return : a new beginning for Yellowstone National Park / Celia Godkin.
Description: Toronto, Ontario Canada : Pajama Press, 2016. | Summary: "In 1995–96, gray wolves were
     reintroduced to Yellowstone National Park to control the elk population. To researchers' surprise, the
     wolves ended up positively impacting the entire ecosystem and landscape. End matter with further
     historical and scientific information completes this illustrated narrative"— Provided by publisher.
Identifiers: ISBN 978-1-77278-011-6 (hardcover)
Subjects: LCSH: Gray wolf – Juvenile literature. | Gray wolf – Conservation – Juvenile literature. | Wolves
     -- Juvenile literature. | Wolves – Reintroduction – Yellowstone National Park – Juvenile literature. |
     BISAC: JUVENILE NONFICTION / Animals / Wolves & Coyotes. | JUVENILE NONFICTION / Science &
     Nature / Environmental Conservation & Protection.
Classification: LCC QL737.C22G635 |DDC 599.773 – dc23

Cover and book design—Gabriela Castillo
Photographs: Wolf Howling—© davemhuntphotography/Shutterstock;
Bison with Grey Wolves—© David Parsons/iStockphoto
Manufactured by Friesens
Printed in Canada

Pajama Press Inc.
181 Carlaw Ave. Suite 207 Toronto, Ontario Canada, M4M 2S1

Distributed in Canada by UTP Distribution
5201 Dufferin Street Toronto, Ontario Canada, M3H 5T8

Distributed in the U.S. by Ingram Publisher Services
1 Ingram Blvd. La Vergne, TN 37086, USA

*Original art created
with mixed media*

Dedicated to all my readers who enjoyed *Wolf Island* and to Evie, the newest family member.

On a moonlit night, a howl rings out across the river valley. The elk prick their ears. They have not heard this sound before, yet they are afraid.

The howl is answered by another…then another.
High on a ridge, the shape of a wolf appears.
More wolves join him. The pack, now silent,
moves swiftly down the slope to make its first kill.

In the weeks that follow, the elk move from the valley bottom
to the higher, more wooded slopes. The grazing is not so lush here
but, in the shelter of the trees, they have a better chance
to escape the wolves.

In the following months, the valley begins to change.
The tree seedlings, once eaten by elk, now have a chance to grow.
In the space of a few years, aspen trees grow tall in the valley.

Berry bushes are growing back too.

Birds and bears feast on the berries.

Beavers swim down the streams that feed the river.
They find the trees they need to build a home.
They fell the trees by chewing through the tree trunks
with their sharp teeth. They build dams with chewed-off
branches packed with mud to hold back the water.

When deep ponds have formed behind the dams,
the beavers build lodges—beaver houses made of sticks.
Here, they will live and raise their families.

Other animals build homes at the beaver ponds too. Muskrats make homes like beaver lodges, using rushes instead of sticks. Muskrat homes make good platforms on which ducks build their nests. Other birds nest among the rushes bordering the ponds.

A multitude of insects live in the ponds.
They are food for many kinds of fishes.
The fish, in turn, feed other animals.

Otters hunt them in the water, osprey dive on them from above, and herons stab fish and frogs in the shallows. The ponds are teeming with life.

Once the river valley was quiet, but now the air is filled
with the hum of insects, the "Reet, reet, reet" of chorus frogs,
and the flute-like notes of songbirds calling to one another.

Every year, birds fly up the river valley on their spring migration. Before, there was a meadow; now there are trees for the birds to nest in. The trees are home to insects that eat leaves and burrow into wood. The birds eat the insects and help to keep these pests in check.

The wolves prey mostly on weak and sick elk. This helps to keep the elk herds healthy. When there were no wolves, the elk herds had grown too big. Now the herds are smaller but healthier.

Elk compete with bison for food and space.
With fewer elk, the bison herds increase in size.

When the wolves have eaten their fill,
birds and bears come to feast on the elk carcasses.

Many animals benefit from the return of the wolves, but not coyotes. Wolves attack coyotes. With fewer coyotes, their prey—rabbits and mice—increase. The rabbits and mice now become food for hawks, weasels, badgers, and foxes.

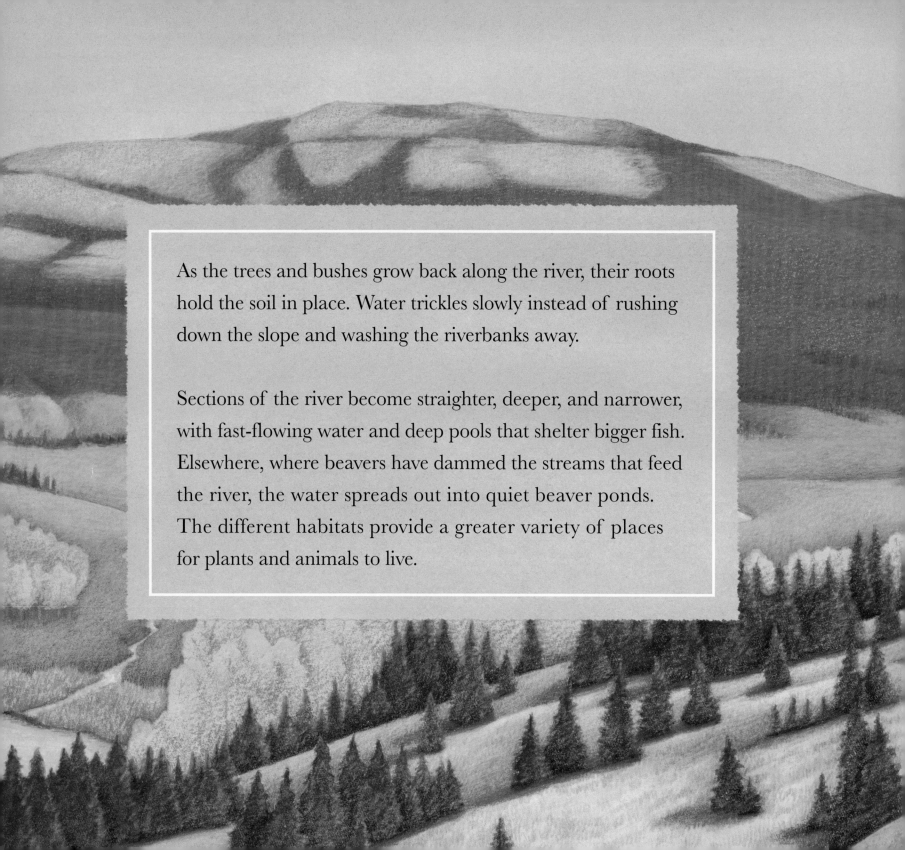

As the trees and bushes grow back along the river, their roots hold the soil in place. Water trickles slowly instead of rushing down the slope and washing the riverbanks away.

Sections of the river become straighter, deeper, and narrower, with fast-flowing water and deep pools that shelter bigger fish. Elsewhere, where beavers have dammed the streams that feed the river, the water spreads out into quiet beaver ponds. The different habitats provide a greater variety of places for plants and animals to live.

Who would have thought that the return of a few wolves could have benefitted so many other animals?

The Wolf
in North America

In the 1800s, as people from Europe spread westward across North America, they encountered wolves everywhere. The newly arrived settlers that wanted to grow crops and raise livestock soon came into conflict with these predators. The wolves preyed on the settlers' livestock and the settlers retaliated by killing the wolves. The wolf hunt was so effective that, by the middle of the 20th century, there were hardly any wolves left in the United States or Mexico.

Over time, people's view of nature began to change. With so few truly wild places left, they started to value wilderness and wildlife. The US Endangered Species Act of 1973 meant that plants and animals under threat could now be protected. In 1978, the wolf was listed as a threatened species in the lower forty-eight states. Many Americans now wanted wolves to be reintroduced to wilderness areas.

In 1995, thirteen wolves, captured in Canada, were released in Yellowstone National Park. The following year another ten wolves were released. The experiment was a success. From the original twenty-three animals there are now about a hundred wolves living in Yellowstone. We have learned that they play a vital role in maintaining the health of other wildlife.

The return of wolves to Yellowstone has had a greater impact than we could have predicted, but wolves are not the only factor at play. Weather conditions, forest fires, insect infestations, and other animals besides wolves may all have significant impacts. Nature is complex, dynamic, and continually changing. We don't know what the future holds, but at least wolves have returned to play a vital role in a place where they have always belonged — Yellowstone National Park.

Pre-European and Current North American Wolf Range

Greenland

Alaska

CANADA

Yellowstone National Park

USA

MEXICO

- current wolf range
- pre-European wolf range
- wolves not recorded here

Author's Note

Most large predators are under threat from human activities. Yet, as the Yellowstone wolves have shown, animals at the top of the food chain play a vital role in the health of the ecosystems where they live. Many other predators, including lions in Africa, tigers in Asia, and whales and sharks in the world's oceans, have similar roles to play. It's time we learned to value these magnificent creatures and find ways to coexist with them.

I am indebted to Douglas W. Smith, leader of the Yellowstone Wolf Project, for reviewing the manuscript and offering helpful suggestions. His compelling book *Decade of the Wolf: Returning the Wild to Yellowstone* (co-authored with Gary Ferguson) provided much useful information. My thanks also to William J. Ripple and Robert Betscha, researchers in the Trophic Cascades Program at Oregon State University, for their invaluable input. Any errors or omissions are mine.

bald eagle

golden eagle

common raven

red-tailed hawk

magpie

gray wolf

jackrabbit

red fox

American badger

great blue heron

long-tailed weasel

osprey

PLANTS & ANIMALS
in this book

yellow pond lily

pond snail

trumpeter swan

blue dasher and
flame skimmer
dragonflies

backswimmer

yellow-headed blackbird

mountain whitefish

water strider

water beetle

redside shiner

cutthroat trout

stonefly